FIND THE GIRL

Find the Girl

POEMS

Lightsey Darst

For MEGAN —
happy writing + reading

COFFEE HOUSE PRESS
MINNEAPOLIS
2010

Coffee House Press books are available to the trade through our primary distributor, Consortium Book Sales & Distribution, www.cbsd.com or (800) 283-3572. For personal orders, catalogs, or other information, write to: info@coffeehousepress.org.

Coffee House Press is a nonprofit literary publishing house. Support from private foundations, corporate giving programs, government programs, and generous individuals helps make the publication of our books possible. We gratefully acknowledge their support in detail in the back of this book.

To you and our many readers around the world,
we send our thanks for your continuing support.

LIBRARY OF CONGRESS CIP INFORMATION
Darst, Lightsey.
Find the girl : poems / by Lightsey Darst.
p. cm.
ISBN 978-1-56689-244-5 (alk. paper)
I. Title.
PS3604.A79F56 2010
811'.6—DC22
2009051609
PRINTED IN THE UNITED STATES
1 3 5 7 9 8 6 4 2
FIRST EDITION | FIRST PRINTING

Thanks to the editors of the journals where some of these poems were first published: *The Antioch Review, elimae, Emprise Review, Gulf Coast,* and *Phoebe.* This book would not have been possible without generous support from the Minnesota State Arts Board and the National Endowment for the Arts.

Thanks to those who've inspired and supported this work, including Corinne Duchesne, Robert Hedin, Greg Watson, the Front Sparrows (Heidi Farrah, Cindra Halm, and Haley Lasché), Chris Fischbach, Trudy Hale (whose beautiful home provided the perfect setting for finishing this book), and the dance community of the Twin Cities. Thanks to Jay for love and encouragement. And thanks to my mother for teaching me all those plant names.

This is for the girls at Fairview Middle School.

11   *Atlantis*

12   *what body*

13   *Debutantes*

14   *1888, London*

15   *Young Gretel*

17   *is your mother*

18   *A few things I learned*

19   *not because I'm dirty*

20   *Methods. listen*

22   *Young Helen*

23   *Thirteen*

24   *House*

25   *for Dawn, for Lila*

26   *still you leave*

28   *Prism*

29   *Fourth of July*

30   *Didn't you hear*

31   *Discovery*

32   *The Drowning*

33   *what's the worst*

34   *Trail*

35   *open & know*

36   *Follow the red silk thread*

37   *Bloody mary*

38   *fill your eyes*

39   *Yde Girl*

41   *JonBenét*

42   *Beautyberry*

43   *Kore*

45   *Tunnel*

46   *Mary, Annie, Liz, Kate, Mary*

47   *Helen, seventeen*

48   *Exhumation. taking you home*

49   *Billboard*

50   *Survivor*

51   *In deep underbrush*

53   *Lantern*

54   *touch me*

55   *Aria*

57   *tell your story*

58   *Snow White*

59   *Search Goes On*

60   *All this time*

61   *Visions*

63   *Highway*

64   *Home*

65   *Unsolved*

66   *Evidence*

67   *Names for Woods*

68   *Azaleas*

69   *Little Snake River*

70   *answer*

71   *Here I am*

72   *need*

73   *forget*

74   *Tell me*

75   *Gretel*

76   *Safe*

77   *Helen*

78   *Digging at Sparta*

80   *Bridge*

82   *Notes*

Your story goes up among us
like wood smoke through trees

Atlantis

Without the roof the walls
stay, but a ruin. The girl gets up, puts on
cutoffs and a halter top, crosses

the street to the gas station and the river beach beyond.
In the water green grass like tongues
wraps around her legs.

She's the kind of girl you can't trust
with even a short note to her mother, fertile
in trouble.   She can wear the dress without

meaning to dance, she can dance
without meaning to sparkle, but why, only a baby
would wait.

Up to her waist and only nine a.m.,
halfway through the long summer. Once she's
gone so far she has to go on in.

*

What is lost is found—in time.

*

A few axioms: follow the lines; piece the edges.

*

I arrive where killers & gods do.
I am a carver, a renovator,
    not a beekeeper. Lucky ones stay away from me.

*

Yes, I've dreamed

finding the women of Irish fable: the giantesses,
    stretched on beaches near monasteries, up
    from the raiding sea with "fifteen ells between her paps"—
    but those bones would break my scale.

*

Meanwhile, these: fine-weight, filigree. Please be patient, I have not
    yet salvaged anything from this ground.

*

Debutantes

Summer & we dance
in our new skins. Jars of fireflies, sparklers:
held fire.

Our sisters the prom queens leave us
their cast-off sashes & tiaras. For dress-up
we wear our mothers' old silk slips—they've never been

smooth as this. We dream
of climbing pines, hand over hand
looking down at everyone. At the playground,

nose to iron, we lick
its hot skin, kicking
to the top of the swingset's arc—metal bolts

rage & our sisters wave from the parade float—belles
as we will be. Silver in their baths, they pluck
dark shoots, they moan, perfume, they sing

hurt anthems into phones—beyond their open windows
a storm of moths, furry green
descending on mock orange, legs creeping, burrow-fat.

Dull afternoons, ground level
we pick apart the fading flower, lay its pulped symmetries
to either side—petal, lip, throat, staining our fingers. Hot

nights we will lie
tucking up our shorts, our little shirts,
pulling the fabric back into the creases. In dreams we climb,

our sticky sap legs and here
is future amber already with its spider,
we are jeweled, shining, pulling back our cherry panties into the creases.

All we have to sell: one
　　　　red ribbon. Belonged
to our sister—we sold
her skirts already.
　　　　Or we have a few songs.

"let a girl wear
lily of the valley &"

Thursday is a dead day, a lost day—you know why.
Friday's full of holes.
eat the fruit only
of a sickly tree
nothing lasts long enough for a diary

　　　　　　　The news is, ladies are being murdered
　　　　by a man who's searching for (kissed me
on the stairs) something he lost
inside them. A pocketwatch? When he finds it
　　　　(ticking) will he stop?

"I'll look out for you
if you'll look out for me"

Our sister dropped dead, nothing catching,
　　　　don't worry. Yellow wallpaper peels
behind your head and you don't notice. Is this
　　　　the man? Each kiss a quicksilver prick.

Young Gretel

Milk-teeth spaced wide enough to suck a lemon ice between.
Crimped blonde hair she tosses—already learning girl,
you're stirring a my-little-pony brand of trouble,
                    not everyone will mistake you for a fairy princess—

your kingdom this box of novels turning dust, your mother's
dingy bras, a drawer of Kool-Aid and its crawling ants.
Your voice already like something lying on its back—
            (behind your mother's camellias hissing *my latest crush*)

*

You lead us back in the woods to see the hobos—
                crumble cake
                        we'll make a trail
We've heard about their camp. Thin October trees
Fourteen is the perfect age (we're nine)

& here is the bend in the path,
the circle of poisonous mushrooms: you turn & run, say you saw
a bent man staring: *vulture mouth*

*

At recess you let boys run you down & kiss you.
            We run hard as we can—we're still fast, we don't
think not to. You say they want

        each girl with her slice, crumbling

to suck milk from *your real ones* &
you're going to let them. You tell us
all you've done & how you liked it. Gretel you know

*

each one's hands sticky, sweet

how to fix a lie
like a pretty picture to the wall (you can

admit it to us, you are
lying aren't you)

Behind you > black slash rises
—back to safety

*

Find the girl in time. Find her
and you stop her future:
*

       always in a sundress she'll spin, always
       in that unbroken field—
*

blue sky of her dreams. Otherwise
she'll be surprised who she turns

this season, passing under ladders causes
harm to growing bodies, let her look up
*

in fear: mountains will be cast down, *we*
must wound ourselves for fresh color,

this wind has scented us.
*

They separated us for sex ed. "Wipe
front to back," the man said, as if he'd tried it and it was easy.
We asked about erections, not about pleasure.

Tell me how you learned, what you learned. I didn't sleep,
crumpled on the floor against boys. Was it fun. The boy
touching my thigh but they were hot thighs, I can't blame him.

Some girls had come in busty and without a chance.
We all had cravings, fingers, throbbing to music.
Then I didn't know it was sex, would deny

when boyfriends asked me. "That's gross." A boy
behind me lifting my denim skirt
with an orange pylon over his pelvis. That year,

everyone sprayed White Rain hearts on walls
and lit them. Girl parts in cross-section, colored in and
scratched out. We remembered everything we'd been told.

                                every hour
a separate arm pointing at a brick wall: close your thighs.

You want to be popular where breath comes easy, the table
full of pretty girls sucking milkshakes, giggling. But
storm and a hole in the ground you can't see from here—

suddenly you fall in, shamed.   Days of thinking
        you're a lesbian or a saint, God's apostle
        sent to vomit at Fairview Middle School.

Here in the valley of hate and yellow busses. Dying
to get sick and stay home and *I'd say let anything wreck*
that low shed now but it's where you live, small version

of myself. Secret notes, arrow-folded,

sad as a galaxy of their own. No one listening.
We argue abortion, slap hands and sing, but it's real
this slashed-face time. Don't think we're nothing but children.

19

*

Find the girl in time and she doesn't
wind up in the newspaper with her feet

photographed bare sticking out from under
a rhododendron bush.

It's real, the bad men who know already
where they would hide the body crouch

in shrubs under her bedroom window
while she talks on the phone.
*

You could say there's a betrayal in my work. Offer me
a wrist, I'll pass you some names. Offer me an ankle,
*

I'll unfold
            "almost like murdering her again" / to
*

unpack, to sift
the varied dirt of her, notes & shreds

of *listening in to her princess phone weren't you*
when she made that date & how can you know which

is the bank of the river to curse & which to bless
without me—

where even to lay your flowers down.
*

But what can today do, a door
is always slipping open in a river, a bridge
*

where a stalled Ford pickup
gleams—
*

Let her suffer it, since someone has to,
some to be the stories

others survive, learn.
*

Young Helen

impossible to remove & therefore remaining forever

        Such a small fate for the one who waits in the hall,
the one who strains against the needling voice of the record,
whose thin shadow caresses
a yellow wall, the one
indelible.

You will be someone's tragic summer, lovesick
moan as the screen door slams again and June bugs
strike it with confused ardor.

Your mother, your sister
leave them on the bed, your gifts—
satin armor & a quiver of swansdown arrows.
They tell you your history: how you burst
from the golden egg, how beautiful you were and will be.

What do they want of you?

Such a small time, the present,
       where the dark pool waits under the battleship sky,
       where the lily is not blooming yet but will,
       where the ice cream truck chimes in the vanishing distance,

someone's daughter running penniless alongside.

Thirteen

Do you remember the first day—
it was waiting for you under a girl's flowered underwear,
as if you'd been dreaming it all along. *I was a crone, I smelled the*
difference.

All that concrete, those eyes, graffiti alive
on its angry wall. So many girls behind plate-glass windows, airless
classrooms, hush, but a valve burst open—we're all thirteen—

wish you could redeem her? She's gone into the small jewels
of your tears, your earrings. That suicide, razor blade hoarder,
cheap candy gorger, relic of the moment when something shifts

under you, the world in seven pieces and you are grasping, rain
and your head barely above water. Draw a thin hair between your teeth.
The doors open in. It will never happen again—that ache, that stain
forever.

The girl's question: why
is it my part to allow / to have it in me
& open that store to others

Ravage—the ragged sound alone appeals to me
      —*damage*: my sacredness my broken statuette

*

Those little girls—how they dress, their eyes
reverberate in mirrors—you unashamed
too young yet to know

I wish I could / have made the opening myself / have freed—

*

And me, said the girl,
I am not a discoverer I am land that must be cleared
from under brambles or cloud cover.

I am not hard-headed anymore, I found out
at a small cost
but why is it no one thought to tell

*

Broken cockle our mother,
did you think it was better this way—a wound so deep
an amputation hidden with a bandage /

I don't want to say it hurts
but it is a place where past and future have been buried
with their secret razors

It is not my fault she will say
to her half-grown insubstantial daughter
that I still perceive myself as a sewer

for Dawn, for Lila

You race the fifty meter dash gun
    to zero, by girls with blade legs, flower names.

Science notes: structure of blood & human ovary,

                    trace around *I love I hate*

We slide off our skirts for dirty gym shorts
scatter grackle-like across cracked ground to the field for
a moment adult then panic gaping
like sinkholes inside & now

you will run around the gravel track quickly without knowing why.

*

Slowly you learn the void. In biology class, girls hyperventilate
on lab tables, hold each others' heads
in the thickening smell of frogs.

Skin crawls. You slit the belly of the frog, find him bloodless.

I wanted to believe we could levitate each other
with two fingers or have visions.

                <what makes you think you haven't>

    once you saw the truth: blackberries grown over it

Girl it will turn out well.
All the bridges you'll cross scrawled
with graffiti you don't know you won't write.

        oh you'll be happy. it cauterizes where it burns that power

25

Heart & lungs, the queen demands.
*

Going through woods
means the girl has come of age. Did you screen her calls?
*

I'm tired of smiling at men, she said. The lost-
and-found of common speech, I dig back up &
        what corrosive sweets were you feeding her?
*

wolf's rib / The microscope's grip on her is one infallible thing. Tell me
*

your dirty jokes & ghost stories—I archive as I've
been taught the folklore of this region. *How do you think mother it came*
*

by the name beautyberry? She said the graffiti sang it. I rarely get
a live one. The man who eats women, "Well that ain't so,"

and the woman who confronts him with a gnawed hand, "It is so,"
at the church picnic—good, isn't it, my latest mountain tale.
*

No, I can't help you. Those were her secrets, she won't file charges,
the face has lost its smile & even a sample is helpful. Red fabric

caught in azalea crotch—you dressed her this way? I've uncovered
the face of Helen—whole, meanwhile every digging yields another scrap
*

of this one. Remind me to ask about that older sister—peroxide
flash in the woods behind the house. *I love*
*

my family I am so happy she said. *The water is over,* she whispered,
does it mean anything to you? Her words don't amount to much—
*

no data. Only a few of my cases are beautiful. *in a dream*
her bare finger pointed to
*

don't interrupt this investigation. With art I knit
bone to bone & no one will not say she looks alive. Another
*

clue you've missed: these skeins of stems pale
in their green breakage confirm she came this way.

Storm-eyed in algebra class.
On the bus swinging by crosses hung with plastic morning glory.
Stadium lights thick with moths & so little sound.

The past's option   [*you could have*]   shrinking
        into a mineshaft's *no* / air stilling, smearing

that cobalt poison over,
                under the eye that saw this
        trivia: shadowbox scenes of her
first sex, mother's kitchen, the bright mobile
        of angelfish swinging over her tiny bed at night and when she first bled

the shark turning his hammerhead
slow in the water below

A bonfire and we dance
Nothing scars us: we're
        safe, just kids, because one girl gets <   >
        —under oak trees a strange end—

"oh she lives"—
But everyone gets groped
        by boys who say they love us, fingering
she cries in homeroom but she's a slut. We aren't: everything

    we hold tight / sharding apart
        throat closing / is there
any other way / this wrecked house and each dark fold into

the dress before
why don't we hide in our lockers / get drunk / how good

(*we are*) do you have to be
        before they'll melt your nails for soap?

Didn't you hear

               Followed her home
"she didn't see him"   "saw & didn't care"

               > in his cellar, above blackberry jelly, the highest jars
               are flush with shorn-off women's hair. ("he eats them")

                              apples on a stick make me sick
                              make my heart go two forty six or

thought she was lucky, running with him
to a mattress in the woods & as her mood ring catches the light
       / her beautiful friend's body

*

Orange vests on, we join the search.

—stumble across fields in neat rows
tracking her for the clue is dropped & now from this black rock

we fan out like starlings.
(our ribbon baskets alert to receive

rich bones)

*

girls who sit like this get this like this (snaps)

his car & she watches scenery go by (pecan stands)

*

And if I find you
we will have only minutes for you to tell me

before the men come with their black plastic bags
                    <she-dog nibbles a rib bone

*

I found the girl. Don't hear glory: I like to dig.
*

I dig between lines of white string—unmeshing
your cosmos, tunneling. I like to uncover, pick out,
*

rearrange. I like to dissect & to flesh. Then I remake.
*

I found her wound in strips of cloth, perfumed, dry,
her organs—stomach, liver, rosebud ovaries—sweetening in their god-
head jars.

I found her in the ancient city,

level c, bundled beneath the dust of her family, first to die.
There they folded bodies under beds: her little sister
*

slept over her in dreams of poppy fields.

I found her headless, cast in bronze and two ton, sixteen feet under
cerulean waves.
*

I found her

*

    with shovel and toothbrush
    by the Green River shore

    slim ulna & radius
    your charm bracelet still
*

The Drowning

And the cutting off of air—

confession aching to come, I did x
& I am guilty / I was
a little believer once & now no cure

*

Let me warn you: you will be given gifts, made to think you are unusual.
      I was proud to be alone, the smart one, first
of her kind, to what extent (please answer) do you feel

you are the product of a sexist system—Athena
in cold marble: I sat for that pose too.

*

Bitter however of it
hanging in tall trees: I am not going to provide
        anything for you / so on the other side you rise,

      hands red with luck, but I won't have helped you there—each
her own disease / I see

your claws scraping
inside your tower window / silently

*

I didn't sleep last night

a barrier is as a barrier does sweet hemorrhaging saint
suffocation like plague in dark boxes it rained all day

said the girl and I'm not waterproof

Now & Later's, Milk Duds
Sweet tooth, the man at the counter moans
you got a real sweet tooth legs
taffy-whips under fluorescent light

[*dialogue*]
       so girl: what do the boys call you
       will you believe what they call me
                    I believe you
       you won't believe me

   *

                     they'll bury you in pieces if you let them see you that way
—"right through me
like a gap in landscape"
       Sick of getting licked—this sugar-girl melts.

my aches, I said, Please, Dr. Johnson,
       it doesn't feel right *and he said,*
       then we'd have to test your sexual parts. I'd have
       to reach in there

   *

Hey baby want to suck my dick
           viper voice seeping from the cracked window
           of the house near you that is always for sale
    —tomorrow I'll wear something flashy /

mother do you know how it is to be called slut?

       yes I do "My best memory from middle school: in the bathroom
they painted pink to make us tranquil, splattering
       wet paper wads like soaked pads on the ceiling"

Trail

The woods are green, the path winds
through blackberries.

You dream of his hands on your thigh,
you dream of his hands on your neck.

You follow
a narrow path, can't smell
him up ahead, the bear, nose
deep in arbutus.

But always his breath
on your throat, his hand, his mouth.

You will eat the blackberries, listen
for the tremble of clear water
on mica-flecked rock.

You dream a cataract, an edge. But the bear prowls and eats
on the far side of the river.

*
Unlike an amateur, I can tell wolves from girls.
*
The thigh bone is a giveaway; the pelvis is better.
A little hair and we're all set. No you're never

standard issue by the time I see you: bees in your hair, string
*
around her wrist, teeth in her ribs. Faces
smashed or pristine, pure as the tomb or ligatured & bloat—
*
Quiet: it takes days to see one strand of white-blonde hair
among these trays of numbered bones. Still I know it's her,
*
your daughter the distance runner, by this splintered shin—
this dental mark this faint tattoo. So turn in all your shreds

of her, those garbage bags of arid facts. *I'm afraid oh I'm afraid*. I found her
in a bone gulch, a field so blue, a burning car, her bracelet
*
in a drainage pipe, her right ear in a broken jar—her death mask
in an antique store, her coccyx filigreed in gold. Fine weather
*
means ten days, foul means five, the river
means never, and you love possibility I know. I love
*
the round knobs of femurs settling in smoothed sockets,
I can tell you this, you're still. These symbols,
*
to you arcane, to me gospel—logos
of a toe-tag. A groove listened to for clues—so trust me,

I ransacked her drawers & her diary, fingered those perfumed
*
& giggly entries. What can you know of her that I don't?
I have looked inside her chest her head her womb & seen the vacancy.
*

35

Beautiful as a plum, my girl—
& just as keen to be bitten.

Mother will you keep her in

On a vase she tumbles into the arms of the god
of underneath: "he will crown me in granite & ruby"

Sweet thing, you have made it all simpler
& more brightly colored,
lovely through your kaleidoscope,

but
  Do you think
    I went too far, the dead girl whispers, her nails
    scraping down your window, her skinless smile—

The sister: You will take, take, eat.

 "She stepped into the clear trap,
  she picked the wrong rose, alarms
  of bees & earth
  swallowed her whole."

Yes. Persephone you plummet, no one smiling as he lifts
his iron sickle your braids falling in wheat heaps

If you open it little parasite little tick
digs in, cyst
drains loose &

inside you a hazelnut skull grows.

"flushed that blood slip
& back to the school dance with a slick down her thighs"

*

Black walnut stain under arching trees.
Erosion. A sinkhole, weak crust above, step
& it spoils, this thin limestone—

& drifters sleep at the base of the sinking, their fires
(what chars in those fires)   Witness: this hollow is you:
fresh-edged, jagged; others
          smooth by now, their sides
          wallow in Cherokee rose.

*

< "can't stand this"—fungus unfurling,
          curdling, on downed trees.

Are you weaving a sack for your dreams
to drown them in like blind kittens   Listen:

voice of a black widow in the small
vulva of your ear, crying
& singing her can't go song

37

*

She will be *aren't they all* desperate for my grasp. Sweet scent
of flowers long past prime—fence her father put up

around that precious roseyard. Everyone is afraid. You can climb
over child I said *I need more & you're plumbed,* found
*

lacking & I can fix that my little cripple my depth cure. To prove
*

she's a sacrifice, I seek something distinctive: six lines sliced

or violets growing in her hand. This one will never tell
the truth. If I ask you a question if I move your jawbone
*

for you blow through the hollow church of your neck will you
*

answer. Then *this is the story, exactly as she said,* I would announce.
You *a pattern rain makes coming across a field*—

but that pattern is the sign of something underneath—no wonder
they stripped, tore, burned to know. *Every morning another story*
*

on the milk carton, alert on the interstate billboard—you've got to
look hard, a waitress at Denny's says

she spotted that girl eating onion rings, you've got to
listen closely for police bulletins, she might be
*

starving, stealing in the candy aisle, crying in the crawl space
of the house next door, she might be you—
*

Yde Girl

Digging, two peat harvesters unearth
a shrunken but still human form: their shovels bite
into leathered skin, her body winces and the red force
of her remaining hair shakes free, teeth

a grin rattle in her sucked-out face, and the peat diggers run,
crying *demon*—
      Their own kinswoman, their dead aunt,
planted by their fathers.

    *

Picked from thousands: heroine, we are
only taking your body: you have been
lying here for years already, a twisted
and rank witch, your heart a dry fish.

Lucky one, your hair shimmering
in the hang of rich centuries,
your arms full of ravens—we
will change them to doves.

    *

think you'll find her smiling asleep in her old bed
                    in this diner, a sign
                        with her name & picture, a nickel box

            and a man stares hard
                as he downs his coffee but is he
recognizing her or just scratching his itch.
*

Ritual sacrifice—a magic common once but not today.
The victim strangled and stabbed, twice-killed
not from cruelty but to make sure.

                    to breathe again under peat, dark
                      stinking crush inside a mouth—

    *

think you'll walk down the old path
  and there she'll be kneeling, saying

        I am ready, take me home
        I've learned, *I bring back secrets*

*

Today someone loves her enough to remake
her face with his fancy equations—sixteen years old,
hair tumbling (blonde, before
the bog) in Barbie waves by the side of her head

                        as if she were your daughter
              or someone you knew

*

      you can dress her, soothe her,
            make her feel fear

After she was found & before the scientists came,
local people pried loose her teeth
and one finger bone

                  something to hang for luck, to save us
                        this body gone holy with time and murder
out of that sack of a face

*

            Is she praying for you
                  home again and whole

                  or is she an angel & better this way
*

You, made goddess: hidden source, pinned here
and choked below us

poor leather girl, cipher,
with your rag of red hair

      were you ever alive to be killed

40

JonBenét

You're smoking in the alley when I see you next—
those thin cigarettes your mother died on.
The little pageant winner in her red sash

if she weren't dead would be almost as old as you. To steal, you reach
with your crushable hand past that thin angel
smiling from the Walgreen's checkout, still,

maybe for one last time, with eyes as blue as Crater Lake.
You have all the world if you'll forgive it—anything you
want, all you need to do is take hold.

*

This isn't over. The girls are waiting
for a sign, *it's safe*
on a satin flag. Her fingers have not forgotten, will

go on scratching, skin under the nail, a clutching bone
naked/   You didn't want to be the girl anymore, wanted
to grow up, be what comes next, the lion.

That one—like you she'd be a runaway by now, gone plain, wire-scarred
and where she got away, a few evenly spaced holes. A girl is a woman
is a rack to be hung with gashed sky, take it off me you say

*

The turnpike overpass where you've huddled / your life
an animal caught in a trap. Your life
a wrecked arm your life standing

a few feet away in a parking lot. For a dead girl she's lovely,
but you haven't seen how we found her. The body a sack
for the working system, liver & lungs and a scarab heart.

A fern pressed in a bible,
found years later, marked evidence a. You smoke to be ugly.
The eyes' blue an accident, hot breath, all the gray clothes of the sky & lightning
ribbons.

41

This line of her arm
we carefully trace as if fossil
of a new-found water creature.

An instrument built from her body
we made harp-pins of her little finger bones
harp-strings of her long yellow hair

plays one song / Hands

rotted to ruby leaves
so much richer now.

Oh the wind and rain
An amethyst vein opens
bladderpods rattle and
devil's walking stick

pierce me / The house of the murderer will stand
where the stream running from this crime

stops singing.

*

I am tired of remembering: listen—
Girls just like her but fleshed troll the intersection below.
*

The speed of summer precludes me from offering any guess—face
of an angel naturally I'll say, angel eroding from every pore.
*

What the locket is, the scratchy voice on the tape has said,
this can be analyzed & brought home

to the puzzled, grieving family. What her silence is, no
single anchor or print can prove. Tell them,
*

each flower is laden with its brilliant color, but no
not with its color, the fuchsia

erupts between eye & petal, and so beauty, even
like hers, is pixel, wind current, & some few triggers in

the victim eye, staggering at curve, line, sapphire iris & fair hair.
*

This bone doesn't do her justice: make a flute of it.
This mind doesn't hold the scene: *certainly officer*
*

I saw the man talking I know he had no business
to but did I study his height? no. his face?

no. his eyes? Sir, I was busy watching that seductive infant myself.
*

Her recovered arm
shows bruises—caressed too forcefully & he can say

I didn't realize how little love a frame like that admits
*

Girls in orange in season are a cinch to hit
as they comb the woods for trillium. Nothing more to say

43

of this: pinned
against the barn wall forever in her same pose
*

Tunnel

She calls
for help, but> girl in your red
apron (sexy thing): ethics elsewhere—an old man

who is a thinker denies
her right <you wish you were
dicked & armored> instead of vulnerable, loose> budded> less than

shadow on a dove
eclipse wrecks us. when you think well
of your own work, you're <fucked> thick with graffiti> not good

<girl you went under the street through the tunnel to save a
minute in a short skirt that's the price you pay on the other side you
come up staggering into the flower markets and kilt stores
of Dean St.>

Mary, Annie, Liz, Kate, Mary

>   tell me "you spring from nowhere
>   love & will peel fresh as a flower"
>   *from these witching woods*

You left us nothing but names and dead faces,
the names men called you, faces
twisting away.

Your bone corset, blue-trimmed coat,
jay-feather hat, your old chemise, all
burned in rusty smoke.

I survived, I got out, I'm telling you, I'm whole. Whatever
became of the others—hair swirling with mine in the photo
as water in water, fall, bright mountain leaves, far from here.

You followed a red trail to a narrow door—lifting
your petticoat so its stains were seen, a scar already there,
begging—You are

the ungenerous ones,
our ancestresses, to leave us only this,
this path, this market.

I said You must be the killer by your clear blue eyes—
so sit with me

Partridgeberry each twinned drop of it: the need
is real, these redcaps sewn for these sleek girls, red corsets
   to conceal the strain.

At Café Risque: *Will my kid sister know me in the blurry*
 shot by the queenly way I turn my heel?—I hope I hope.

  The smell
draws men fast as   *chain fern and copper fern, maidenhair*
 and bindweed   these names don't forget them, they matter—

I see now: the gifts are burning holes
through us just as the giver knew they would.

—what was I doing when it fell apart the first time / women
  cupping their broken hands to catch / sister,

     you told me I couldn't keep
the red embroidery and clear water / apart

On my trail in these woods I keep seeing
pieces of bodies like mine strewn
and bees humming to visit them

*

Gin-pony Liz, too late to pose in that flower hat: Jack waits
with his scalpel & I with mine behind him. What evidence
*

do you think I need to know you? *I have seen*
the goddess's face in dreams. Throw it in the trunk, that torso—

one butterfly bone will tell me. *All those nights, mother,*

brushing my golden hair and for this. Dear Liz, I could tell you
of their nightlong laughing—you would never believe

how they howl in their banshee boxes. & still: I enter
*

the mystery this way: I savior myself: I am
taken into the shade of their marrow am ruled
*

by the arriving constellation of those bone homes.
—But I must keep shut or I'll
*

give away the quarry, as-yet secret site where we
are still digging them, knee-deep in ancient gold.

The princess's fading crown of thyme atomizes in our sun.
See, a clean slice was possible: her chiffon & satin untorn,
*

no skin waiting to be pried & no testimony
in her falling face, no trace of history.
*

Billboard

The 2007 peach queens of Clifton County welcome you
to this stretch of kudzu & jack pine.

> *I am not your impression of me*
> fly in amber, struggling, ruined wing.

Below their smiles
a stand for pecans, the beaten trees
bending, arching in neat rows.

> *I am not the flat version.*
> *I am not the thin version.*
> *I am not the one held together with barbed wire.*

You can gather
your own berries
in these long hot fields—the handwritten
sign in blue.

> *I am not the one* hanging
> with one hand
>   onto the tailgate of the black truck.

> I am not the bas-relief, I
>   am not the photogenic swamp.

> I am not the good sister.

> I am a peach queen, I am welcoming you

Hurricane at Saint George:
            shells empty by the time they rolled to you,
    polished peach-red insides / every day

          we escape someone doesn't
  life for ours   like you I've gone
      dangerous places, walking down Frenchtown alleys

        and the cross on the way to school is telling you
no one will know. there are always holes, mossy ravines   you've trusted

          strange men and dark rooms   do you think
   you're different   the one who survives, the golden one

          fresh from the leaf pile & shallow grave
  back from the peat bog with hair still growing and bright

My life a candle, waiting
for a match. I wasn't sure
I'd flare—
but we all burn down the same.

What's happened to me—
my skirt's been slit and I'm wearing it,
next door's maniacs and I've spoiled my religion—
. . . and other items: you'll listen,
      won't you

*

This door leads into a witch's house
(glow in the dark stars).

While practical blackbirds smirk from power lines

girls in locker rooms
shriek, black nail voices & stellar
      graffiti—   *slut   bitch whore*   *Lonnie Rd Girls*

—just a thread
you can pick up & follow out to a highway where a black van no trees for miles

*

Yes, I was a virgin, I noticed that.
(It ought to have been surgically destroyed.)

Trim the wicks, girls, wash the globes
of your lanterns. There is a work, it is simple. But if
you break the glass, a blood cut, you are (did you want to be)

*

lost.

51

"everyone dreams / of intervention"

Sudden summer hail. The all-night drugstore
is where you find her, sweet meteor so bright
luna moths mob her their long green tails the prettiest
almost the prettiest thing she'll ever see.

Not here either—followed the fireflies.

A time-enhanced photo
may be sent to all parents, the missing at age eleven, crooked teeth,

jumper with one strap mussed, last seen
in the company of herself and her dreams, climbing into

a semi bound for Mexico, making her getaway

with all she has in the world packed
in her Snow White lunchbox.

*

I only follow; I only abide. *I think they should pluck out his eyes*

Is it the spine whispering
to me through its broken and trivial hangers

—gods buzzing around you in obsidian jewels

your shadow like several crows or hands converging
on cash or feed

& that lovely compartment inside you, the one you promised
to everyone, is it still rich with brocade & emerald & gold?

Kiss me—I only reveal you where
you have forever & fevered to be, & you shriek at last there,
*
in the place, under my hands, turned to yourself your last ounce.

> *I wanted bones to cry out to me from the earth—*
> *
> *on all sides, thin bones*
> *that were mine only—*
> *
> *girl-bones that knew my hand.*

I knew I was dangerous: razor in a soft fruit
                                    this is
            the everlasting he said *between*
                this finger and this neck

I knew I'd walk out of the killing forest whole
    knew I'd been lost a long time, face-up
< chainsaws argue over the dead tree, sap gems

            I'll be rich in amber
*

All is stinking & deepening its rot around us—
but you see nothing.

The key, string
spindle, web, kiss

apple, bandage, barrette, cotton anklet
bite of cake grackle on the line the hours rings

we wear clawing the shadows that block our ways all
nameless one instant

I wish the earth bare myself a throat & nails only so that
you might hear this, I might dig myself screaming

free from the moss and the grapevine over me & my call
yes heard though miles away & through a young girl's fever dream.

*

The scene of almost rain, almost
disclosure: how many times the hunter

stepped close to her body before
the skull rattled loose with his spent shell

Cleaning knives after her kill. Shreds of our Easter dresses
on barbed wire fences *girl go back go on going back down there*

*

This? A skull with roots
tunneling where once there was a dream.

They corkscrew like her hair—in these melodramatic recreations.
No, I never fear for my daughter. You needed so little—almost
*

a houseplant, "just let me go"

and you would find your way home
through fields and woods in your thin shirt

and torn red skirt. And never need another taste?
Bend close to my shoulder, I'll show you where Kate Eddowes lies
*

rose by moonlight, opened eyes, covered
in florets, scarlet centers he's razored

from her Queen Anne's lace. *I've done
my best to make you holy*
*

What makes this work difficult is the
/ no this is sacrifice, not murder—see the merciful edges

[Sometimes I think violence inspires me] Here
*

I go again cutting.
The family will want to know, not

know / about the last minutes / was there time
*

All causes are equal
All cases are equal

*I've been sent dogs to identify, police said they're children. A man skeleton
in a dress they thought was a woman. Natural deaths and old, old burials.*
*

57

do you have
            scars / if not the hurt is mostly imagined.

slash of blood against snow and who would wish for a child
"red as blood"—pretty words,
but the daughter suffers.

When I was young I loved _____, now
I love _____, and in between
                salt air, eclipse, the tinny rust of each year's puncture.

"As white as snow as red as blood" —I'd include more news

            if I knew it. For she was a thin little thing,
hardly more than a peep coming from that carmine mouth—

                yes ma'am, I'd like to bite the shiny apple, please.
A disease will fill the airwaves until spring and then a girl

and then a war. "And black as ebony." Mother,
you had your wishes, all three. And then you die and she

            is running through midnight woods while
                the most beautiful woman in the world
            salts and peppers the heart & lungs she leaves behind.

Search Goes On

Body might
be abducted five year old: search
goes on your wrecked semi standing over you, her
father—you can shiver, you're alive
Don't worry we won't stop uprooting trees for her
                                        loved skin taken
as a shirt you were that close
to being crushed, daffodils
will bloom in spring in these woods—petal-orange tape
marking where we've been / All

under the decaying trunks more decays,
leaf-mold and click-beetle, grub and centipede
trickling away into fern, wood rotten into dirt, worn
and pale-blue fungus like bits of flesh. Rhododendron flower

and girls are still alive in the mountain town
nearby, sharp-toothed ugly girls hiding
behind jars of candy sticks or carved clocks.

tick> I've been gone a long time, look how
the postcard in the mail shows me aged five years, you don't
recognize me tock> you won't. Not when I
sell you rotten apples, pray for you, or wave you gone.

*

A gray yes of sheer risk. Every broken cornstalk witnesses
your shimmering existence but this steel table extends

in all directions, bleak, slick as video, littered with the mending & cutting
instruments of my trade—slit

out the pockets, cysts of her illicit silence—fish bones,
hide of a lamb draped over a snake cage for an asphalt heart, my
*
neon mainstay—always lovely
no matter how the rain may pit and pock you.
*
"No wonder—could not even name the flower
over which she fell."

Meanwhile, at the pageant she would have won
*
you are closer than skin to this truth. A valley

several miles from the city is where we lay them, side
and jeweled side by side, and being there

is not like remaining yourself in a room with more windows
*

Visions

                                              light as a feather stiff as a board

Once we lifted one even threw her high
but she was skeleton already & the bits of her
flew and scattered across the stars. funny

What she saw: boys at a sinkhole laughing
              Her mother a girl / an old woman
              Her sisters braiding, embroidering
              her prom dress / nurse sewing it closed

              She whispers, "I am in fields now"
dried all one yellow so the blue
of your eye will find you out, radiant
as a flare above the site of the kill
                            [her last vision the culvert

    *

I could poison the aquifer.
          : a jawbone in the rain for weeks—learning to speak
          your language

or that screaming quiet & decorous, wallpaper
of roses, lavender, without thorn
                        I know they're sharp, I can't help
                                    my bones
                  > little chunks falling off by the wayside, in the red phlox

"some nerve damage, some dirt
permanently rubbed in your hair my dear"
                        —so I find
                        no more crumbs to follow.

    *

Finger through these helpless pictographs: her comb,
poison bottle, curve in an otherwise-clear river

let headwaters weep on me
And when I come back

I'll spare you
yes I'll
        merciful"

                            —As always she smells of honeysuckle; bright
                            day of the finding

I have loved all day and all night
sexual sign, sticky promise / you gave the promise
you think a girl is an angel

"you know he killed her family to get to her"

the sign of sin, he says / a saint is a girl who dies young,
before you know otherwise
think we were born impenetrable? *wasn't you*
wrecked her, left her bleeding

you think she's drinking milk in a stationhouse now

you think she won't lure you one day,
silent smile, ghost-thin arms / untouchable survivor:
she's been taught a new lesson

Home

Come home honey
We've had the light on all night & left the porch door open

Mom, I
only walked ten feet I / believed
the signs I never would have cut
these holes in myself. Dad

who warned me of my own emptiness / who
told me of my / everything

I lift already broken into

   grab a knife and consent

*

It's not my affair to judge, I just take notes. "The police thought
she ran away—so we lost the most valuable hours." And she believes

her sister's dead but maybe was alive that night—
her sister who would be forty now. Lady, I have to be sure
*

you haven't buried her yourself in the cellar—so

much more common than masked men—or behind
the rose of Sharon that was her outer bound. Her sister's car—

yes, we found that: cars are too large and permanent to be long lost.
Are you sure you had a daughter? splotch of thigh, sample's
*

by the time they're ready to show you

corroded beyond testing. *Sorry dear sister.* You know
the answer: interred already but not buried. I can put

a hand together with its dimestore chain by color and the jagged
*

hacks of separation but your rib cage—pulverized. I am afraid
that flame, essential, saving shape—   *they're gone*

there is nothing to identify. I can't help you—you see
she lacks defensive injuries, she is still alive. At seventeen
*

what has she done. At twenty what won't she do. These splinters
her fears, these hairs her dreams. I give you all there is.
*

> *don't care was made to care don't care was sorry*

First he gave me apples, then
he gave me pears,
then he gave me sixpence to kiss him on the stairs

    and when it did bleed, the blood did
              come *my waist my stockings my last good skirt*

You made this palace
    rich with tinsel gold,
    flammable, a cigarette girl with her smile
    could set it off   *sir*

two thousand years I've worn your slipknot faithfully &

    please sir remember
    the dole the little maid earned

            "Well that ain't so and it shan't be so
        and god forbid it should ever be so."

> *These are all my words*

"It is so and it shall be so
and here I've got the hand to show"

Names for Woods

Call me Nola, she said,
but she carried her real name safe
under her lapel
        with a twenty she kept
for a taxi.   They asked,

but she kept the name
of her town a secret too, the latitude

of its falls, and the liquid words
she knew for the leaves that turned
        that time of year.

Maple, sweetgum, tupelo,
when force drains the alley
                to black and white and leaves
        sumac that singes the mountainside,

a jacket, one sleeve torn away,
        underneath gray graffiti
        that sings,   *this turning is all*

We burn down
        the homes of whores
        my home, and

I will go there

Azaleas

to have her chest opened so the heart could be seen

Yesterday I found blood on my sheets
for the first time in years. Felt like being
a girl again, to strip first
the sheet I'd slept on, then
the mattress cover, finding how
deep the stain.

When I hid in the closet playing
hide-and-seek my heart
went on making noise
though I willed it to be still:

hidden in those games I gave away
all of myself, peeling
layer after layer;
I thought I had no limit. One night

I was not found
until my mother called me in. By then
I'd opened everything

to the azaleas.
Fuchsia and red,
flesh-scented bloom, they never
gave me back.

Wildflowers: columbine, woodbine, rue, & ironweed.
These hands have long been asking the question

What was it that (every evidence erodes
            in time) soft
        tissue *my lips, my face*

I was cutting flowers I was picking blackberries
a pharaoh's daughter a hooker a suicide

        the identification carefully made and
yes this is my fleshless grin, what was under it
(sweet girl)

I have worn ivory and cold river stone, teeth
    and enemy skin

        the dogs have been at my leg bone
        the dogs have been at my arm bone

All that I am, channeled in slow rot
& sinking further into this alien architecture
    of the inside

                I listen to a man whistle, a strange man breathe
        water falling out of the sky

fourteen years

*

If after all this silence nothing is heard—
my lovely scalpels dulled to rosehip use.
*

I make only the necessary outlines, take
only the necessary dust.
*

Her bones
mixed like several bad animals, this

is not your daughter
but a heap of crows. Was she feathered?
*

Did she survive. Inclination of goldenrod & sun's apex
that afternoon, the bearpath she

unwisely tiptoed & her rusted grommet &
the known molester in his shotgun shack
*

& this picture of her thighs—leaves me
cold and certain she's no more,

though all we uncover is a broken branch.
I will pinpoint
*

only the necessary. Was she beaked? Here
I have strung these crows,

articulated them in the shape of a girl.
Can you bury it, will it do?
*

Here I am

Face of an ancient lady pulverized by light.
You reach
straight through my chest for my golden zone.

Each animal of the zodiac in filigree
but my skin my skin tearing

& you preach as if your breath did not rot
my beautiful breasts, my lips.

How I left—you trace me, marvel
at my missing rib my extra vertebra. Am I
one thing? one cancer one slashing
so beautiful so young one self-immolation,
slit wrist, slaughter?

& fire:
there's nothing smooth about this steadily approaching past.

*

Stars sewn inside hipbones—you don't find.

You don't find
what you come for because I palm it, swallow
in my wind rattle, digest it in the stomach
still curdled in my Canopic jar.

The ground full,
we turn to constellations.

*

I say to the sweet face,
*

I'd talk to you if I could—but no: I'd name you. Strap
    of metal with a date & I'd seal you. I open

    the bone & air the marrow only

to snap shut. I listen, sift, tell
& then all is solid again.
*

But should I whisper—
    that first hour in which you hung

    in a river's quicksand, all
    but the tips of you / horns of you
*

hidden—but whole & fixed all along—
*

You'd like me to make a sound or two.

The mouth flowers: effluvia
                  efflorescence

   I don't need to talk, don't
      need to know how this could have been otherwise, don't
            need to blame forgive or see > I need

to go on making my sweet mistakes, corroding rotting but

The nails: among wild geranium

    sister, moving

[Tell me]

You of the clear eyes, tell me a story
    it will be about girls who lost their way / let
  them lose their way in an autumn wood

   The policy of the crows is always against us
      Let it be the ground that keeps bringing them
back to themselves—Virginia creeper

   finding its way through sockets
you've come home they say, you've come again
       and *body from out the grave* but no one's

    going to put his hand in that slit to test /
  What god has divided let no man put together
her shin bone and her shin bone
    Let there be

    rows of dim apple trees *I refused*
to identify the body it wasn't me you see
    I would've known myself anywhere, even after

   all those years
(my funeral) we will steal our bodies
    from any eyes
  I can feel myself coming free from the history you record

*

Forgetting the directions through the old fir forest, she
*

action of a thing hidden: neuron, woman's sex
   —fiddlehead still tiny, furled in a spangle of dew

The eagle tells by the look in her pupils (thinks he tells) but Gretel's
learned (already) to cry one way as she aches another
*

Poundcake, she whispers, crumbling it
—of course I want to be happy

But dirty pigeons scrawl after the eagle; home's so
*

far in the woods now it's winter already: snow on red berries

Gretel: the path's scar cures as if never made, can't go
back now

but on the other side if you are good you may find your sweets)
*

hunters tracking downwind of the witch, her eyes
two falcons already

free of their jesses   Gretel
*

do you tell by the fear in the wolf's eye or by the heat: approaching fire
this my territory half ruined did she cry

witch's sweet home dismantled, still the reek
of her singed hair Gretel
*

why is it always in the woods you go
never the open field
*

Scrape up my shaven hair,
braid it, hang it
in a corner

Look, girls, a wrecked horse / Remember

the white cat in the story /
cut off her head to be human again—

A remembering place will be sore, we come back scared
from the well where *the other girl* is calling *help*
me up out of here help me but there's no rope or she's
too weak to climb or won't—spider-leg hair hanging & eyes
that glint like a cat's

   /I have only told you true stories,
   /I have only told you good stories.

The horse is dissolving, gently, gently,
he has nothing and never did to do with us,
his bridle is fading into ox-eye daisy and sourgrass,
his veins a loose net sinking into every dewier morning, catching nothing,

   I forgot she didn't cut her own head off she told the prince to do it

and the wide eye-spaces
riddled each night with country stars, heart empty
& emptier, silkily its boundaries fading, the wishes
& the measure of fear slipping from her smooth form,
the uncovered inside of ribs and legs, what was unknown
but beautiful all along.

Helen

No city where she stays
can be defended.
They plead but still she shows

her body in saffron silk to the enemy,
a shape inside a shape moving
like a foal still unlicked from its birth.

Her breath alone tears holes
in Troy walls. Look
at her, cool & leaning against the fragile railing while

all around her, arrows—
but nothing can hurt you with a scar that gold, eyes
flat as asphalt. Her afterimage burns.

The war over, a woman's veil
torn from her face makes front-page news.
She's freed, they argue, gone from the garment,

or is this what's left, would she be
a pale boy on a dusty road
that leads out into the unconquered country

without it. No wonder rumors
of what she did after roam the world,
that she went home a queen, died happy,

followed a dark trade to a narrow door,
took the remnant
cloth and climbed inside its woven skin.

*

We found armor no one could wear,
five-hole cuirasses and gold loops

a yard long, bone pins
no slit or hand would fit.

We found strange jewelry in Helen's grave,
a double-faced bronze-link veil, an earring

that stretched eight feet and anchored
in a second hole, as if (in this sketch

by the reconstructionist) she had two heads,
a wingspan, a hook through the sole of her foot.
*

Here, in this double axe shaped
by two halves of a broken pelvis, rested

her secrets, a spinning universe
and the liquid void that nursed it.

A force has made fossils
where once there was a woman.

Pairing then, two bones by two bones,
their craters and streambeds, we make

the jointed legs of an ancient animal walk—

I sound
the bowl of Helen's cunt with honey, smudge

with a smoking rosemary bundle her aligned ribs.
Bolt and wire

will sink the fake wing

to the shoulder meant to hold it,

while jay feathers singly glued to a skull
and tethered bees re-create her hair.
*

Bridge

Then: trees unfold their colors
in the deep river gorge.

I saw an owl in woods
growing night, embraces
backlit in second-story windows.

How deep, I asked my mother—I had
a long way to go, didn't know it. Every hill
some old man's knuckle—names

seeming natural then, mine, yours, all
of them—history, old women and trees. I listened
to June bugs climbing light (find them

spent under it in the morning)—didn't know
I was a girl then, red leaves in my tangled hair & here
is the joining zone, where anyone becomes anyone

else: how old were you, when the winged shadow
flashed between you and desire, and one organ
that never ceased began pumping?

Notes

1888 is the year of Jack the Ripper's string of murders in the Whitechapel district of London. Mary Ann Nichols, Annie Chapman, Elizabeth Stride, Catherine Eddowes, and Mary Jane Kelly (all prostitutes) are the Ripper's generally accepted victims. Flower and Dean St., in the Whitechapel district, is connected to the murders.

Young Helen: the epigraph is quoted from the Encarta World English Dictionary. Helen of Troy, daughter of Zeus, was born from a golden egg; her sister Clytemnestra, daughter of a mortal man, came from the other egg laid by her mother. Helen later caused the Trojan War, but she had other adventures as well. Greek writers do not agree on her actions, her character, or her fate.

still you leave an outline: Snow White's wicked stepmother wants the huntsman to bring her Snow White's heart and lungs as proof that the girl has been killed. The huntsman has mercy. But he has to bring the stepmother something, so he kills a wild animal, whose organs the wicked stepmother happily eats.

The archaeologist Heinrich Schliemann claimed "I have seen the face of Agamemnon." He also discovered jewelry that he called Helen's.

Discovery: at Catal Huyuk bones were buried in shelf-beds.

The *Yde Girl*, a bog body, was found in 1897 near the village of Yde in the Netherlands. She had been in the bog for approximately two thousand years.

Kore: the image of angels coming from pores of a body is borrowed from Dana Levin.

Beautyberry: In an old song, a harper makes a harp from the body of a drowned girl. The harp plays only one tune, which is "Oh the wind and rain." This song incriminates the killer.

Touch me: The killer's wish is derived from Katherine Ramsland's *Inside the Minds of Serial Killers*.

Unsolved: "by the time they're ready to show you that / they're gone" borrows from Katie Ford.

Azaleas: The epigraph comes from Jan Bondeson's *Buried Alive*.

Safe: The image of the other girl comes from the film *The Ring*.

Digging at Sparta: If Helen went back to her husband after the Trojan War, then she would have died at their home in Sparta. However, other stories exist.

Other sources include Brian Alderson and Helen Oxenbury's *Cakes and Custard*, William Lynwood Montell's *Ghosts along the Cumberland*, Richard M. Dorson's *Buying the Wind*, L.B. Taylor, Jr.'s *The Ghosts of Virginia, vol. IV*, and Douglas Ubelaker and Henry Scammell's *Bones: A Forensic Detective's Casebook*.

Originally from Tallahassee, Florida, Lightsey Darst is a writing instructor, dance critic, and dancer who lives in Minneapolis where she curates a writers' salon. *Find the Girl* is her first collection of poetry.

COLOPHON

Find the Girl was designed at Coffee House Press, in the historic
Grain Belt Brewery's Bottling House near downtown Minneapolis.
The text is set in Minion.

FUNDER ACKNOWLEDGMENTS

Publication of this book was made possible, in part, as a result of special project
grants from the Jerome Foundation, and from the National Endowment for the
Arts, a federal agency, because a great nation deserves great art. Coffee House
Press receives major operating support from the Bush Foundation, the McKnight
Foundation, from Target, and from the Minnesota State Arts Board, through an
appropriation from the Minnesota State Legislature and from the National
Endowment for the Arts. Coffee House also receives support from: three
anonymous donors; Abraham Associates; the Elmer L. and Eleanor J. Andersen
Foundation; Allan Appel; Around Town Literary Media Guides; Bill Berkson; the
James L. and Nancy J. Bildner Foundation; the Patrick and Aimee Butler Family
Foundation; the Buuck Family Foundation; Dorsey & Whitney, LLP; Fredrikson
& Byron, P.A.; Jennifer Haugh; Anselm Hollo and Jane Dalrymple-Hollo; Jeffrey
Hom; Stephen and Isabel Keating; Robert and Margaret Kinney; the Kenneth
Koch Literary Estate; Allan & Cinda Kornblum; the Lenfestey Family
Foundation; Ethan J. Litman; Mary McDermid; Rebecca Rand; Debby Reynolds;
Schwegman, Lundberg, Woessner, P.A.; Charles Steffey and Suzannah Martin;
John Sjoberg; Jeffrey Sugerman; Stu Wilson and Mel Barker; the Archie D. &
Bertha H. Walker Foundation; the Woessner Freeman Family Foundation in
memory of David Hilton; and many other generous individual donors.

NATIONAL ENDOWMENT FOR THE ARTS

This activity is made possible in part by a grant from the Minnesota State Arts Board, through an appropriation by the Minnesota State Legislature and a grant from the National Endowment for the Arts. MINNESOTA STATE ARTS BOARD

TARGET.

To you and our many readers across the country,
we send our thanks for your continuing support.

Good books are brewing at www.coffeehousepress.org